Know your Pet

DOGS and Puppies

Michaela Miller

First published in the UK in 2006 by
QED Publishing
A Quarto Group company
226 City Road
London EC1V 2TT
www.qed-publishing.co.uk

This edition published in 2007 by Silverdale Books
An imprint of Bookmart Ltd
Registered Number 2372865
Trading as Bookmart Limited
Blaby Road
Wigston
Leicester
LE18 4SE

636.7 MIL

Words in **bold** are explained in the glossary on page 30.

A Catalogue record for this book is available from the British Library.

ISBN 978 1 84509 491 1

Written by Michaela Miller
Consultant Chris Laurence, QVRM, TD, BCSc, MRCVS, Veterinary Director of Dogs Trust
Designed by Melissa Alaverdy
Editor Louisa Somerville
Pictures supplied by Warren Photographic

Publisher Steve Evans
Editorial Director Jean Coppendale
Art Director Zeta Davies

Printed and bound in China

The publishers cannot accept liability for any information or links found on third-party websites.

Contents

The right dog for you

Dogs make wonderful pets. They love to play, walk and run with their owners and be part of the family. But dogs can also be hard work, so think carefully about what's involved before you decide to give a dog or puppy a home.

It's your choice! Labradors come in three colours: chocolate, yellow and black.

Is a dog for me?

To find out if a dog is the right pet for you and your family, here are some questions to ask each other:

🐾 Will we be happy to look after a dog even when it is sick or old?

🐾 Will we take it for walks twice a day even if it is wet and cold outside?

🐾 Will we make sure that the dog is never left on its own for more than three hours during the day?

🐾 Do we have an escape-proof garden so it can play outside safely?

🐾 Can we afford to pay the vet for our dog's yearly vaccinations and for any other care it might need?

🐾 When we go on holiday can we afford to keep our dog in kennels, if we can't take it with us?

If you can answer 'yes' to all the questions then a dog could be just the pet for you!

Dogs, dogs, dogs

Dogs come in all shapes and sizes, from tiny Chihuahuas to huge Great Danes. They also have different **temperaments**, so try to choose one that suits your family. For example, a large boisterous dog such as a flat-coated retriever or Border collie may not be good with small children, who could get hurt if knocked over. A smaller dog with a calm and friendly temperament might be better. As well as pure breed dogs (see page 9) such as Labradors and spaniels, there are lots of mixed breed dogs – or mongrels – which make lovely pets.

Big or small, long or short-haired, there are so many types of dog!

Dog or puppy?

Puppies are very appealing, but they need a lot of care. They need toilet training and obedience training and can also be messy and destructive. Adopting a fully grown dog from a rescue shelter might be a better choice. Although these dogs may take time to settle into a new home, they can make excellent pets. Before making a decision, why not get some advice from a vet?

On the Wild side

All dogs are descended from wolves. People began keeping wolves as pets about 10, 000–15, 000 years ago, to protect their homes and herd their animals. Although this was long ago, learning about wolf behaviour is helpful for understanding how your own pet dog thinks. It can also help you to care for your dog properly.

Different characteristics

After the first wolves were taken in and cared for, people started breeding them to have different **characteristics**. Dogs such as collies and sheepdogs were bred to herd farm animals. Some dogs, such as golden retrievers, were bred to find and retrieve (fetch) birds, or other animals the owner had hunted. Others, such as small poodles and Chihuahuas, were bred simply for companionship.

Wolves normally walk about 50 kilometres a day in search of food. Your dog won't need to do that, but its instinct is still to keep busy. This is why regular walks and mental activity help to keep your dog happy and healthy.

Wolves howl when they are separated from other pack members and to warn wolves from different packs to keep away. They may also howl when they have hunted down their prey.

Part of the pack

Wolves are social animals – they live in groups, known as packs. Like a wolf, your dog is a social animal and it needs a pack to make it happy. Your family is your new dog's pack! The dog needs to learn to have good relationships with the other members in the pack family, including accepting that it must do what it's told. If your dog doesn't learn how to behave when it's a puppy, then behavioural problems such as jumping up, growling when it shouldn't, biting and aggression can develop.

Border collies are bred to work herding livestock, but in the right hands they can make wonderful pets.

How do dogs communicate?

Dogs have their own body language. An aggressive dog stands with its ears pricked up and head held high. It will stare, bare its teeth and make the fur along its back stand up to make itself look bigger. It will also growl or bark and hold its tail straight out. If a dog is frightened, it may **cower** with its ears flattened and its teeth bared. It might whine and whimper. A friendly dog has its eyes wide open and its mouth looking as if it's smiling. Happy dogs often whimper or yap, too.

Do you want a pure breed or a mongrel? If you want a purebred dog, you'll need to find a specialist who breeds and sells them.

Training a puppy takes time and effort, so you might prefer to get a grown-up dog. Look in rescue centres, although a rescue dog may not be trained the way you want and you may need to spend time re-training it.

Purebreds

The Kennel Club, which represents breeders from all over the country, is a good place to search for a purebred. Most breed clubs have websites that will help you find breeders in your area. There are also websites for rescue organizations that specialize in looking after purebred dogs. Don't buy puppies through advertisements offering lots of different breeds. These may be dogs from puppy farms which do not breed responsibly or care for their animals well.

An eight-week-old Alsatian puppy enjoying a game.

8

Good puppy practice

Before you buy, make sure you see your puppy with its mother to get a good idea of the size of dog the puppy is likely to become. If its mother seems happy with people, then your puppy will probably be the same – if you bring it up properly. Choose a puppy with a clean nose and teeth. It should have no signs of diarrhoea around its tail and should walk without limping. If you are buying from a breeder, the puppy may have had its first vaccinations and they should also give you a diet sheet so you can give the dog the right food.

Pet shops sometimes sell puppies, but it's not a good idea to buy from them. Puppies from different litters are often kept together. Mixing puppies in this way, before they have had their vaccinations, means there is a high risk of your puppy becoming very ill.

What is a pedigree?

Pedigree is another name for a pure breed of dog. Pure breeds are created by mating male and female dogs that share certain characteristics, such as colour, type of coat or temperament. When they're old enough, the puppies are then mated with each other or with other close relatives. It usually takes about ten years and eight generations of dog to create a pedigree. Any pedigree puppy, or dog, that you buy from a breeder should have a certificate and registration document from The Kennel Club.

Adopting a rescue dog

Animal shelters are excellent places to look for dogs and puppies. If you and your family are thinking of adopting a rescue dog or puppy, ask your vet to recommend some local shelters.

Rescue dogs can make very good pets but make sure that you choose one that will suit your family.

Asking questions

Good shelters will ask you questions to make sure that the dog is going to the right home. Most shelters also do home checks to make sure that you, your house and garden are right for a dog. You should also ask about the dog you'd like to adopt. The more you learn about it, the better. It would be heartbreaking to take a dog back to a shelter because you find that it can't get on with your cat, doesn't like small children or is scared of cars.

Pet payment

Most animal shelters expect you to make a donation or payment for the dog you take away, to show that you have made a commitment to your new pet. This money usually goes towards paying for some of the care it will have received at the shelter.

Most dogs and puppies that end up in animal shelters have been taken there, or abandoned, because their owners found that they could not care for a dog.

What is neutering?

Neutering is an operation that stops dogs from being able to produce puppies. There are so many unwanted dogs that it's a good idea to get yours neutered. Neutering can help to prevent some types of cancer and other diseases as the dog grows older. Vets will advise you on the best time to have the operation. Dogs from shelters are usually neutered before you take them or, if it's a puppy, you may have to take it back to be neutered when it's old enough.

Getting ready

Before you bring your new puppy or dog home, make sure that you have the right food and equipment ready.

Feeding time

The breeder or animal shelter should tell you what food your dog is used to, so make any changes gradually. Dogs of different sizes and ages need different amounts and types of food. A three-month-old puppy, for example, will need four meals a day of special puppy food. A fully grown dog may need feeding just once a day. Your dog must always have fresh water available and its food bowl should be washed out daily.

Collars and leads

Without a collar and lead it is hard to train a dog to walk safely and to behave well. Your puppy will need a soft collar that's loose enough to fit two fingers between it and the puppy's neck. You'll also need a lead that clips on and off easily.

Check with the breeder or animal shelter about the right style of lead and collar for your type of dog.

Bed time

Your dog's bed should be a non-chewable, rigid plastic basket that can be easily cleaned. Any bedding should be washable, too. The bed should be in a quiet place and never in an area that can get too hot, such as a conservatory. Some owners put their puppy's bed inside a big cage or crate. The puppy learns to treat the crate as its den. Once it's used to it, your dog can be left inside its crate with the door shut for short amounts of time when necessary. Crates can be a safe way to transport dogs in cars.

Make sure that your dog's basket is not in a draughty place.

Car travel

When you bring your puppy home, and for its first trips to the vet, it should travel in its crate or in a well-ventilated pet carrier. A dog can travel on the back seat of a car if wearing a harness attached to the seatbelt, and also in the boot of a hatchback if secured safely. Never leave your dog in a car on a warm day, even in the shade with a window open. Temperatures in cars rise fast and your dog could die in just a few minutes.

The first few days in a new home can be quite a stressful time for a puppy. It will miss its mother, and its brothers and sisters and it will have lots of new things to get used to.

Gently does it

When you bring your puppy home, first take it into your garden or yard so that it can go to the toilet if it needs to. Then take it to the room that contains its bed, food and water. Sit quietly and let it sniff around the room. Your puppy will come to you when it is ready. Make sure it goes outside after eating or drinking to go to the toilet. Don't let your puppy go beyond the garden until it has had all of its vaccinations as it could catch a disease.

Crate training

To introduce your puppy to its crate make sure its bed, water and a toy are already inside. The adult in charge of training should say 'Into your crate!' in a cheerful voice and give the puppy a treat when it goes in. Leave the door open so it can leave at any time. Soon the puppy will go in and out of the crate quite happily and treat it as its special place. You can then close the door for a few minutes at a time.

Toilet training

To help puppies go to the toilet in the right place, always take them outside when they wake up, after they have been playing and after eating and drinking. Give them lots of praise when they go. A three-month-old puppy will usually need to go to the toilet every three hours. Dogs and puppies should never be shouted at if they accidentally go to the toilet indoors. This will only make them more nervous. Simply say 'No!' firmly and move them to their outdoor spot.

As your puppy gets used to its new home and owners, it will relax and become more confident.

Meeting other dogs and cats

If you have a crate, leave your puppy inside for short periods and give any other dogs or cats you have a chance to get used to the new arrival's look and smell. When you let the puppy out, don't leave it alone with other pets until they are comfortable with each other. Be particularly careful introducing an adult dog to other household pets. Keep it on its lead. It can take a few weeks for animals to get used to each other. Don't leave them alone together during this time.

Grooming gets rid of dirt, loose hair and dead skin and helps to keep a dog's skin in good condition. It also strengthens the bond between you and your dog. While grooming, you can check for fleas and make sure that your dog's eyes and ears are clear of infections.

Brush work

For long-haired dogs you will need a soft brush and a bristle brush, wide and fine-toothed combs and a stripping comb. Groom a short-haired dog with a rough mitt. Brush gently along its back and sides in the direction that your dog's fur grows, then underneath its tummy and around its tail. Comb long-haired areas and tangles very gently. Older dogs sometimes need to be washed with dog shampoo (but bathing too often can be bad for their coat).

Different types of dog have different coats and some will need longer grooming sessions than others. Long-haired dogs such as Afghan hounds, Yorkshire terriers and golden retrievers need daily grooming.

If you aren't sure which brush is right for your dog, ask your vet.

Handling tips

Stroke your dog along its sides rather than patting it on the head, which most dogs see as a threatening gesture. Don't encourage your dog to jump up and lick your face – you could be knocked over. To stop a dog doing this, keep your hands by your sides and walk past it. Once it has stopped jumping, tell it to 'Sit', then praise it. If it keeps jumping up or pawing you, don't look at it and leave the room.

Tooth brushing and claw clipping

Brushing can make your puppy's teeth last longer by stopping plaque building up. It can also stop bad breath. Tooth brushing should be done by an adult, using special toothpaste and brushes, which are available from pet shops. Most dogs' claws wear down as the dog walks, but if they grow too long, they need to be clipped. Let the vet clip the claws the first time, so that the adult in charge of the dog can learn how to do it without hurting the dog.

Training matters

Training a dog properly is very important. It teaches the dog to behave well with humans and other dogs. Untrained dogs can cause problems. They won't come when they're called, they pull on their leads and may try to attack other dogs or even bite humans.

One adult trainer

Although the whole family should make sure that a dog behaves properly, one adult must be in charge of the training. If too many people are involved, your dog will get confused. Once your dog understands the basic commands taught by the adult, you can start to use them and join in the training, too.

Short and sweet

The best training involves a system of rewards and praise when the dog or puppy does as it is told. If it doesn't do as it's told, no reward is given until it does. Don't shout at your dog or punish it. Keep sessions to between five and fifteen minutes long because a dog can lose concentration easily. It's usually best to train your dog when it's hungry, as it makes it more eager for treats.

Teaching 'Come'

Start this session in a quiet room with you and a trainer.

1. The trainer divides one of the dog's meals into five to ten portions.
2. The helper holds the dog gently by its collar.
3. The trainer stands a short distance away from the dog with a portion of the food in their hands.
4. The trainer then says the dog's name and calls 'Come' in a pleased and happy voice.
5. The helper lets the dog's collar go. As the dog comes, the trainer should start moving down to its level, while praising it and showing it the food.
6. The dog should be given lots of pats and strokes and allowed to eat the food. Repeat this exercise until all the food is finished.

After about a week you can start asking the dog to come to you for a simple treat and then after that, just for lots of pats and praise.

Outdoor training

When your puppy or dog is fully trained indoors, the next step is to teach it to come when you are outside. This can be harder, as there will be more going on outdoors. You'll need an extending lead and a toy or a dried dog-food titbit to use as a reward.

Your dog's favourite toy can be used as a reward.

1. Say your puppy's name and call 'Come'.

2. If the puppy doesn't come, jerk the lead lightly to get its attention and try again. Don't use the lead to pull the puppy towards you.

3. When it comes, give the puppy lots of praise and a reward, such as a toy or dog biscuit.

20

Training your dog to sit

Once your dog knows the command to come, you can try teaching 'Sit'.

1. Call your dog towards you using 'Come' and show it the food treat.

2. When your dog is in front of you, move your hand containing the food over its head. It will try to keep its eyes on the food and will start to sit down.

3. As it does this, say 'Sit' and give the treat. Once your dog has learnt the command, you can then train it to respond when you say 'Sit' from the side, front or behind.

When your dog understands the commands, you won't have to give so many treats – the words and praise will be enough. When you give food treats, be careful how much you give. Training sessions should not make your dog fat!

Lead on

You must teach your puppy to walk on a lead. First, let your puppy get used to its lead. Clip the leash to the collar and leave your puppy to walk around the house for short periods of time.

Walking on a lead

The first step in teaching your dog to walk on a lead is teaching it to walk to heel.

1. Start with the dog in the sit position – on your left side is best. Make sure its lead is kept quite short to keep the dog close to your body. Hold the other end of the lead in your right hand and a food treat in your left hand.

2. Start walking. Say your dog's name and then 'Heel', keeping your dog close to your left side. When it keeps to heel for a few paces give it a small treat. Eventually your dog will make the connection and stop trying to pull away.

Furniture and food

Don't let your dog lie on furniture or beds because it will think that it's in charge, not you! Your dog could become very difficult to train and may start behaving badly. Don't feed your dog until after you have eaten and never feed it from the table. This will also help you to keep control. An adult should be in charge of feeding the dog.

Learning to walk to heel is the first step in training your dog to walk on the lead.

Playtime

Playing games is fun for both you and your dog. It's also great fun choosing toys for your pet because there are so many different types to choose from.

Choosing toys

Make sure the toys you choose are well made and safety tested. If your dog chews bits off the toy, throw it away and buy a new one. The pieces could get stuck inside your dog and require an operation to take them out. As time goes by, you'll get to know which toys your dog prefers!

Chewable toys

Don't give your dog old clothes or shoes to play with. It won't know the difference between clothes that are toys and those that aren't and will end up chewing your clothes, too. Large rubber chew toys that can be filled with healthy food treats are fun and they will stop your dog from chewing clothes or furniture. You can also buy chews and rubber, nylon or sterilized bones from pet shops. Just about all dogs like bones to chew!

Sterilized bones are best because they have been specially prepared so that they don't contain any bacteria that could make your dog ill.

Other toys

Some dogs like twisted rope toys that they can pull on. A ball is good for playing catch and fetch. Throw the ball away from the dog rather than towards it, in case the ball gets stuck in the dog's throat. Frisbees also make good toys. Never throw sticks for a dog as it could be injured if it accidentally runs onto the end of the stick.

The adult in charge of training should give the toys out and pack them away after play. This will help to stop dogs becoming territorial and aggressive about their toys.

Hide and seek

Have a game of hide-and-seek with your pet. Tell the dog to 'Stay'. Show it a tasty treat or a toy and then let it see you hide it somewhere. Then say 'Seek' and let it find the treat. Next time, tell the dog to 'Stay', show it the treat and then pretend to hide it in several different places. Say 'Seek' and make a big fuss of your dog when it finds it.

At the vet

A veterinary surgeon will become one of your dog's best friends and an important source of dog care advice for the family. Look in the phone book or ask neighbours who have pets to recommend a vet in your area.

First visit

The first time your dog should see the vet is for a health check within the first two days of bringing it home. This is the time to ask for advice on neutering and vaccination against diseases such as **parvovirus** and **distemper**, which are catching and can kill dogs. Your vet will tell you how often your dog should be brought back for its **booster shots**.

Lost and found

Your vet can also microchip your dog and register your name and address on a database so that if your pet is ever lost, it can be returned to you. A microchip is as small as a grain of rice and is painlessly inserted under your dog's skin. Many animal shelters, vets, dog wardens and police stations have scanners that can read the chip on any lost dog that is brought to them.

Fleas and worms

Your vet can treat your dog for worms and fleas. Regular worming is important because dog faeces can contain Toxocara (roundworm) eggs, which can cause blindness in humans. Dogs can also suffer from other roundworms and tapeworms. If left untreated, worms can make your dog ill. Your puppy should be wormed every two weeks and an adult dog about every three to four months. If a dog is scratching a lot it may have fleas. If so, ask the vet for a treatment to get rid of them.

To stop disease from spreading, the adult responsible for your dog should clean up after it, even if it has been wormed.

Fleas are brown parasites that run through a dog's fur and feed on its blood. They can cause rashes and infections in your dog's skin and can infest the whole house.

When is a dog unwell?

Take your dog to the vet if it seems unwell. If it is uninterested in its food, favourite games and toys and is sleeping a lot more than usual then it could be ill. Other signs of sickness include runny eyes and nose, diarrhoea, vomiting, difficulty breathing, limping and difficulty going to the toilet.

Just like elderly people, elderly dogs usually need special care to make sure they stay fit and healthy for as long as possible.

Tooth and claw

An older dog needs to be taken to the vet twice a year for check-ups and to make sure its vaccinations are up to date. Your vet will check your dog's claws — when dogs get older they exercise less and their claws can overgrow and make their feet sore. The vet will check your dog's teeth — and possibly clean them too — because dogs can get a build-up of **tartar** on their teeth, which can cause infections and loose teeth.

Extra comfort

As dogs get older their joints may ache, so extra padding in a bed will provide comfort. If your dog gets very stiff your vet may prescribe pills to make it more comfortable. Sometimes older dogs find it harder to see and hear. You can help them feel more at ease by not moving furniture around. Stick to regular times and routes for walks to make your pet feel more secure.

Saying goodbye

If your pet is very ill it may have to be put down. This is when the vet gives it an injection so that it dies painlessly. Afterwards you can leave its body at the vet's or bring it home to bury. Your vet may cremate your dog so that you can scatter the ashes. It is very sad when a pet dies. You may find it helpful to write a story, look at photos or make a scrapbook about your pet's life.

West Highland white terrier

Labrador

Afghan hound

How long do dogs live?

Small and medium-sized dogs, such as Jack Russells and spaniels, usually live to be about 15 years old. Larger dogs, such as Afghan hounds, live for about 12 or 13 years while very large dogs, such as mastiffs, rarely live beyond 10 or 11 years old.

As it gets older, your dog may like to sleep more. Leave it alone to rest and it will come to you when it is ready.

Glossary

booster shot   An extra shot of vaccine to keep a dog protected from disease

breed   A group of purebred dogs that share certain characteristics, such as coat colour. Labradors and Airedales are examples of breeds

characteristics   Features such as colour and length of coat, temperament and abilities

cower   When a frightened dog lowers its body to the ground

distemper   A deadly disease that causes high temperature, coughing and a runny nose and eyes

neuter   An operation that stops a dog being able to produce puppies

parvovirus   An infectious disease that dogs should be vaccinated against

tartar   A hard substance that can build up on a dog's teeth

temperament   The way that a dog behaves

Index

Notes for parents

Dogs and children

Owning a dog can be a wonderful experience for the whole family. However, it is also a big responsibility. Although this book has described certain dog care tasks that children can be involved in, the adults in the family are entirely responsible for the dog's wellbeing and the safety of children around it.

You should be certain that you can afford all necessary veterinary, training and kennel bills before getting a dog.

There should also be an adult at home most of the time, as it is unfair to leave a dog on its own for more than three hours a day.

Dog ownership can benefit children greatly as it can teach them about loyalty, responsibility and care. However, there are safety rules that you need to bear in mind to make dog ownership as enjoyable as possible.

Safety checklist

- Dogs need to be walked twice a day. The adults in the family should take responsibility for this, as it can be dangerous for a child under the age of 16 to keep control of a dog.

- By law, you must take responsibility for cleaning up your dog's mess when you take it out for walks. Dog faeces can spread disease.

- To protect young children from being knocked over or bitten they should not be left alone with a dog, and only adult members of the family should feed it.

- Do not allow a child to carry food near a dog, as it may try to snatch the food and knock the child over.

- Children should be taught to stroke their dog – and any other dog – from the side and not from the front, and never to pat its head. Head patting is a dominant gesture that can make some dogs snap.

- Train your dog to lie down and stay when young children are playing together. If children are playing a game of ball and the dog tries to join in, the children could end up getting hurt.